Desire.

The Cornerstone between nothing and Success

MICHAEL TABIRADE

First published in Great Britain by Michael Tabirade, 2018

ISBN: 978-1-9997804-1-8

Printed and bound by CreateSpace, a DBA of On-Demand Publishing, LLC

To get in contact with Michael Tabirade, visit
www.michaeltabirade.com

DISCLAIMER

Everything in this book; the articles, reviews, information products and services, is aimed at improving, developing, and enhancing the hearts and minds of an individual to achieve their desired outcomes and more. The information from this book has been gathered from psychology, self-improvement, project management based information, primary and secondary research as well as observational findings. As assured that I am that these teachings and principles have worked for me, I cannot guarantee that they will work for you but it is well-known that success and obtaining real positive change is dependent upon many factors such as your level of skill, competence, mindset, perception, dominant environments, emotional and social intelligence, as well as many other varying factors. Change is heavily dependent on you and nothing in this book can promise or guarantee change, however, I hope that you realise the change within you so that you can make the first progressive step.

THIS IS DEDICATED TO THE INDIVIDUALS FIGHTING HARD TO TRANSFORM THEIR DREAMS...

CONTENTS

The starting point of all achievement is desire

— NAPOLEON HILL

Knowledge is the eye of desire and can become the pilot of the soul

— WILL DURANT

Desire.

PREFACE

What is Desire? It is a real deep rooted hunger to achieve a specific goal or task. Many align it to passion, but at its core it is a recurrent and almost perpetual-like feeling of wanting. It is a recurring feeling of ill-completion. Those identified as great in our society have attributed much of their success to it. But those amongst us who do not share the stage with these great people, don't seem to have it in mass. The question is "how do you get desire?" I believe it comes from the following sources:

1. *Adversity*

Many of us have been in situations that have manifested scenarios where our resilience has been tested. The fact of the matter is we either fail or pass those tests. There are some individuals who endure pain in such a way that it only impresses a lesson upon them. There are others who get lost in their pain and they remain in that space. The ability to acknowledge adversity, no matter how long or short, and learn from it, is one where the potential for greatness can be born. In other words, people want to gain more, whilst avoiding pain, and a personal and intrusive experience can ignite the impetus to want to change. How does this work? Well on a very basic level, neurological messages have been fired to your emotional brain and then to your rational brain so much, that you rationally and emotionally need to make a change... From there, desire is born. This of course is theory, however this can be inferred by elements from Ph.D Daniel Goleman's, *Emotional Intelligence: Why it can matter more than IQ*. In layman's terms if something drastic has happened to you, or over a long period of time your mood and well-being is negatively affected, you're going to want to change. The long period of time gives you the opportunity to come up with a rational and initially an emotionally-led decision to change your lifestyle, with the aim of improving your day-to-day conditions.

As many of us use the term adversity repeatedly, I would like to question its definition. It is defined as *difficult or unpleasant situations*. So for you to experience adversity you would need to identify a situation that is unpleasant or difficult in nature. If your native tongue is English, and you have no affiliation with the Ghanaian culture, attempting to speak the Ghanaian dialect Twi may prove to be difficult, however would you call this adversity? If you're a vegan, being forced to eat a double-whopper meal from Burger King is unpleasant but would you call that adversity? I guess what is missing from this definition is "the prolonged experience of difficult or unpleasant situations." This definition highlights an important factor... time. The length of time one experiences adversity is the very reason why one would claim a situation as adverse. This is the case because if something happens frequently over a period of time, it may trigger the message that you have been going through adversity. The impact of an experience is also a factor that contributes to the quality of adversity, and will be explained in the *Events* section.

2. Events

Some may argue that it takes a one-time experience or event that triggers the want to do a specific thing. This event albeit good or bad changes your perspective where a purpose, passion or desire is born. Can you attribute these new perspectives to one event? From a relative point of view, not necessarily. For those familiar with the Law of Compounding, we realise that overtime our moods are affected by the conditions that we have been put in. Each prominent moment contributes to how we shape our experiences and therefore our perspectives. Upon reflection we can make a judgement upon what we conclude of an event. This in essence influences how we respond to related scenarios, or reminds us of these past events, and in turn determines the course of our future. Desire is born when you are able to see every chance and opportunity in life related to your inner want to accomplish a goal. Desire is hunger, the want to consume, explore, have and be more; to have the ability to experience more abundantly.

Experiences and events go hand in hand, but the reason the word "events" is being focussed on is because it signifies a huge and impressionable experience. This is why in the first book *Understand Reach Expand*, you were asked to highlight your hallmark experiences with the aim for you to highlight lessons you can draw from them. When lessons are truly understood you have the ability to add to the fire of desire and work ferociously towards an ambition.

3. Other people's experiences

We as humans do not always learn from our own experiences, but from the experiences of others. It can easily be argued that learning from our own experiences carries with it a higher potency, however there are many people who learn from others. As an example, when we see many people getting burnt by an event whether that be a relationship or business venture, we may be inclined to stay consciously away from it and never see it as an opportunity. If we observe a person of influence going through a positive or negative event, our actions may be tailored to this new form of information. Understanding this gives us the realisation that people affect us whether we like it or not; they are part of our environment. But it is good to note that they can be used as fantastic tools to position us for achievement. They can also be used unforgivingly as a deterrent against our flow of progress.

When it comes to desire, knowledge of someone else's experiences can have an impact on you. Depending on your level of empathy, emotional and social intelligence, you can use this information in such a way that you can utilise your creativity and imagination to encourage yourself to take desire-focused action. The person you learn from could be a family member, friend, colleague or mentor like figure; they may even be someone you have never met before but have read or heard about elsewhere. The point is, the story you have learned about them has a perspective impact on your inner motivations.

All of these sources of desire can be discovered simultaneously, but when at least one is recognised as genuine, it is a powerful force driving you towards your goal. That driver is key, because at the forefront of your mind you know what you want to do and why you want to do it, everything else by definition should work itself out. This is supported by the fact that you believe in the realisation of the goal. Whether it is an actual belief or an overpowering desire is a totally different question, but that inner "need," and motivation is enough to generate a feeling of "it needs to be done and it will be done."

Many of us think we have desire but we don't. These thoughts come into play because books and thoughts leaders have told us that we need desire to win. Although this is not always true, for the most part it helps in the process of achievement. The reason why it is not always true is because depending on how you are positioned in your market, all you may need is a strong enough feeling in order to win, but surprisingly it may not be something you truly desire. An extreme form of desire is known to you and I as an obsession. We need to remember that desire is a feeling, and feelings change as your rational thinking and environments change. However, that feeling is less likely to change if you have managed your mind in such a way to focus on your primary aim. You cannot just get desire, desire comes to you overtime. The more you experience, improve your self-awareness and enhance your ability to deduce goal-orientated conclusions from your observations, the more likely you are to direct your focus to a cause.

Desire is great, but coupled with discipline and organisation it is powerful. Desire makes you good, but coupled with discipline and organisation it makes you great! Harness your power from the desire you feel, and channel your actions in such a way to get focus-based results. Read this book with intent and purpose, and unlock your potential for achieving the invisible.

For further help and guidance on positioning yourself for Success check out http://michaeltabirade.com

Stay connected, stay focused and align yourself for Success.

CHAPTER ONE

PASSION

DISCOVERING THE POWER OF PASSION

Passion is the genesis of genius.

Tony Robbins

PASSION AND WORK DON'T MIX

We cannot escape the activities of work; it is something that humans were designed to do i.e. by nature, we are teleological achievers. The work you end up doing determines the quality of your life, however when talking about work in the aspect of a means, many of us can relate to the fact that we trade hours a week for money in order to make a living for ourselves. Whether we like the work or not does not matter for some, as we are trying to pay our bills, put food in our mouths, and if we're lucky have some form of social life. When working on your passion you may face some challenges and even have some fears, but there is something totally different pushing you forward, and that is passion. It gives you the freedom to endure hard work and face what you must in order to achieve a result. Dr. Maxwell Maltz states in his book Psycho-cybernetics that we have an automatic psycho-cybernetic mechanism within us that when activated against a goal, works independently towards accomplishing that goal when a person has a trusting and relaxed attitude towards achieving it. Executing your passion never feels like work because it generates strong emotional responses that allows you to overcome barriers. Take time to sit down and think about what you do to make a living, is it truly what you want to do in life, does it feel like your passion? If yes congratulations, truly you are an example for society! If your answer is no, are you aware that you have a passion? If you are, what are you doing to work towards it? It is paramount to cut out the rubbish and be completely honest with yourself. People end up in "situations" when they lie to themselves about the life they should live, rather than cross-checking what their environments have hardwired to them based on the conclusions and evaluations they have made and believed about life. Please note that passion does not relate to something big and grand, it's more about how a topic, or an idea of achieving an aim or goal makes you feel.

YOUR PASSION IS YOUR SMILE

Think of a baby smiling right now and you'll smile! If you didn't then the baby you thought of is very ugly or the prior sentence failed horribly! Babies have the ability to make many people smile and feel warm and fuzzy. There is almost a primitive soul-like connection you can relate to with a baby that you cannot necessarily get with an adult. They have an uncanny ability to make you feel happy, and that's it. That moment of happiness you just expressed is priceless because you imagined a scenario that caused you to smile, and it generated a feeling! Imagine if you had that sort of controlled emotional power all the time. This is what happens when you think about your passion. But what is the difference between thinking about your passion, and looking at a baby? The answer is in the question if you haven't got it already... There is a visual, engaging and interactive aid when looking at a baby (the aid being the baby). Imagine using your thoughts and creative faculties to remind you of your passion, triggered by the environment in a natural way. As aforementioned in my book *Understand Reach Expand*, people must use or create something that generates the heightened feeling of what they feel when they experience passion. Remember this clearly, every time you generate a feeling from your passion, you are living your passion. Try this out to emphasise the point being made:

- Think of 10 things you want in your life; if you're experiencing difficulty with this get someone to help you.

- Make sure the person facilitating and helping you does not suggest, or tell you what your wants are, rather they should help channel your thinking.

- The facilitator must be strict, their job is to remind you of how you should do the task.

- Once you have done this for each want, write down on the next page or column why you want it. If this is difficult the facilitator can use the '5-whys technique' to get to the core reason of why you want what you want i.e. ask why with context after you have answered each question. Normally there is a feeling or standard we want to experience frequently related to an event that has usually happened in the past; it is either an avoidance or gift, a pain or a gain.

- Next identify the feeling you will get when you imagine

or even think about obtaining or achieving what you desire. Usually people look up and slightly to the right , pause, and smile when thinking creatively. Some know straight away, others give it a lot of thought. I know this because I have tried this out with a select few.

- Following on from this go back to your wants and circle your top 3, think carefully about what you chose and why you prioritised them.

- Finally, out of your top 3 wants, circle the one that you truly want the most, and see it as priority over all the others.

This is not meant to be a conscious battle, rather a way for you to realise and prioritise what you want from life. The power behind this is that one want is probably what will unlock and unleash the ability for you to achieve the rest of them. This is simply because habitual activities are transferable, even more so when you are working on things that are interesting or you are passionate about. Focus purely on this want because it more than likely aligns with your inner-passions. Once completed reflect over the exercise with your accountability buddy (this will be explained later) and talk about how the exercise made you feel. You can record this session via voice recorder or on video just to remind you of what you said and the expressions you made.

YOUR PASSION COMES FIRST

When you are passionate about something you will do whatever it takes to achieve it in order to complement that wish or desire; apparently anyway. Why do I say apparently? Well, you currently have wishes and desires, have you given it your all to manifest them? If not, then how do you know what I'm saying is true? If you have, then you know it's not up for discussion, you just know from experience that it's true. For those of you who haven't experienced this yet feel as though you agree in some way, why don't you try it? You do this every day when you want to eat cereal, even if it is 10pm at night, you'll go into the cupboard, pour some coco pops into a bowl and pour in the milk and munch! Some of you will even go to the extent of going to your local corner shop and buy the coco pops and milk just to satisfy your desire. Try to achieve or do what you are passionate about and never give up. Apply as much hard and intelligent work as possible. Sounds like a bit of a huge task! What is the catch you say? Well, the catch is you're lazy and you'll probably feel like you can't be bothered, there's also the fear complex which was explained in the my previous book. This shouldn't be as big of an issue for you now, why? Because you would have followed the principles, exercises and techniques in the book to change your life for the better that's why. Remember, whether you believe it's your life or that it was loaned to you, you exercise control over it in your sentient mind.

A side note on Passion

Not everyone can identify with a passion per se and at times it can cause more harm than good, especially when looking for one. Most people discover their passion via experiencing many different experiences, which allows them to develop taste and preference for particular things. This is important as it helps with deciding to **commit to a cause**, and staying disciplined, as you naturally like doing something. I say this to put things into context to help those who cannot identify with a passion. If you don't identify with a one then you are more aligned to finding a "focus." This can be discovered in many ways such as:

- Discovering a skill that you have through time and wanting to use that skill in a specific industry for a specific purpose

- Having a deep interest for something that has been influenced by your experiences and your environments

- Wanting to solve a problem because you have realised no one else has solved this particular problem, and by nature you become "passionate" about solving it. This is common, especially if no one has solved this problem for a while

- Being obsessed about a single idea or concept, and feeling a deep desire to fulfil it in order to prove a point or live a particular lifestyle

Discovering your passion is in the journey. The more you live life, find out about who you are, what you like and what problems are out there, the more passionate you can be about an idea.

CHAPTER TWO

INFLUENCERS

FOLLOW THE PATTERNS OF SUCCESS

Success is a science; if you have the conditions, you get the results.

Oscar Wilde

FOLLOW THE LEADERS AND LEARN

You must have heard by now that the best way to become successful in your field is to have a mentor or coach to follow and study how they achieve their results. My first ever mentors and coaches were my parents, and then gradually it became other leaders of authority, friends, family and teachers. Naturally I got bored with what they were teaching me, and resorted to the internet at a young age. I felt free to dive into an ocean of information and explore subjects and topics that I had never explored before. Even though the internet is such a powerful resource, it doesn't necessarily give you the direction you need. However it did give me the push I needed, the advice from a YouTube video featuring Will Smith's words of wisdom led me to read the Alchemist by Paulo Coelho. This opened my mind, my world, and what I thought was possible. I've always been creatively inquisitive but the crumbs I had left led me towards many books that allowed me to focus on areas derived from the psychological, spiritual and self-help realms. To date (2017) I have read around 200 books on these topics and more. I began studying and focusing on collating and understanding this information that allowed me to perform desired actions to reach my goals. I could tell that these books had themes, therefore I followed these themes and principles to create order and direction. Eventually the ideas perpetuated from these books tailored conversations with different people, increasing my value for networking. It expanded my options and led me to meet people that invited me to seminars, events, and classes. Can you see how things can go from average to extraordinary and exciting! Look at your life and see what compounding spirals you have put yourself in, then make a decision to direct the course of your life in the direction you want it to go.

LEARN FROM FAILURE

Have you ever looked closely at why people have failed in something? There's usually only one answer and that is… they quit. They decided to stop what they were striving towards. Their desire or strategy for positioning wasn't effective enough to keep them on course. If you are not the best at something, or you do not win first prize, find a way to be the best and find a unique way to be recognised in your field. From a young age I had always been an extremely athletic person, partaking in the 100m and long jump, karate, football, and rugby. I was performing at county level at a minimum for all of these sports, or representing a nationally recognised club. Everyone in my environment sought me to be the next big talent in one of these disciplines. It never happened. Why, because my 'why' wasn't strong enough. You could argue that at a tender age, a structure of enhanced support is required in order for you to succeed at a higher level, but again the decisions came from me and no one else. But it doesn't make me a failure, it just shows that I did not persevere in that area in my life.

Colonel Sanders was told "No" 1009 times before he was sealed a business deal to start KFC; how did he do this? Let me ask you a question, have you ever had KFC before and if not have you ever heard of KFC? I'm sure a high proportion of the people reading this book would either agree they have had KFC before, or that they are familiar with the KFC brand. This man asked 1010 businesses to partner with in order to start the KFC franchise. How many times would you market yourself until you got what you wanted? Once and then give up? Maybe three times if you were feeling ambitious? Over 10, 50, 100 times? The fact remains even at age 67, Colonel Sanders was prepared to go on till death. That's what it takes!

DISCOVER THE SCIENCE OF SUCCESS

Napoleon Hill has captured the hearts and minds of many people in his timeless classic Think and Grow Rich. He studied over 200 successful men in his time, such as Andrew Carnegie, Henry Ford and Thomas Edison, and collated their thematic characteristics for success. Here are the following characteristics that Napoleon Hill said you need in order to be Rich:

- Desire

- Faith

- Auto-suggestion

- Specialised knowledge

- Imagination

- Organised planning

- The ability to make a decision

- The power of forming a mastermind

- The mystery of sex transmutation

- Understanding of the subconscious mind

- Understanding of the brain

- Using your Sixth Sense

- How to outwit the six ghosts of fear

He suggests to follow these principles and you will inherit a positive change towards your attitudes towards success and your goals, and further ignite your desire; following these principles has progressively done this for me. If we think about people today, thought leaders like Tony Robbins, T Harv Eker, and Robert Kiyosaki, they have paved the way towards showing us how to become wealthy in our society, both in quality of thought, emotional intelligence and financially. Studying patterns and themes really gives you an awareness behind what we need to do to become financially successful. It is not just about financial success; rather financial success is used as a model to display that inner successes builds its framework. I would recommend that you do the following:

- Go back to your journal

- Write down the top 10 people who have done extremely well in your field

- Read their biographies and understand the context

behind their life

- Find the top 10 websites and articles on your chosen industry and understand what topics are being written about

Get into the minds and hearts of these people, and comprehend their rationale for why they did what they did. If you can really get inside the heads of the people that you look up to, not only will you be successful, you may even surpass them as you will be able to identify a gap and work out how you can make your work personal and unique.

CHAPTER THREE

SUPERPOWERS

EVERYONE HAS SUPERPOWERS

Discipline is the refining fire by which talents become ability.

Roy L. Smith

LET DESIRE TAKEOVER

Let desire take over you, allow the feeling of your deep want to take over your consciousness and begin the initiation of 'Project Desire' as soon as this reigns over you. I love using food examples because everyone can relate to them. There is no way on this earth in the West, where you can't find a way to find food if you were starving, otherwise you'll end up like Marvin… (Sorry I had to do it)! That's an interesting point, what happens when you stop eating for life? Life stops on you. The same thing happens when you don't pursue your passion. Hence, allowing desire to take over turns you into a being with superpowers, you do that bit more to get extra metres, you do that bit more to have more time with loved ones, you do that bit more to ask the person of your dreams out on a date. Don't forget this either: How you feel extends your superpowers that much more. How is your diet? Do you have the body you desire? How are the mental conversations in your head? Look at your time and book in sessions to improve your mind, body, and spirit; find a coach, trainer or expert and ask for their advice or services. If you can't do this do not wait on them, a great way to get started is to develop a focus or mastermind group and meetup and workout, cook or read together. If that is still too much you can always do this on social media in order to inspire yourself and others to get that mind, body, and spirit. Go out and start developing superpowers today!

FOCUS ON ONE THING

Despite making sure that you make yourself feel good in order to get a spring in your step and be activated to perform to your peak, it should also be noted that following one aim, one vision, one dream, until successful will ensure success. I believe this happens because the universe in its raw form is conscious energy. As conscious beings we act based on polarisation of thoughts, therefore what we think and do repeatedly polarises our conscious activity. This conscious activity serves as a commander to the subconscious thoughts in our mind that communicates to infinite intelligence, or in other words the original raw form of consciousness. Once polarisation increases, i.e. your thoughts repeatedly show the same thought patterns, infinite intelligence receives them and responds to your subconscious thought, engaging in events that helps the universe conspire towards your thought desires. The stronger your thought focus, the stronger the actualisation. In essence, yes, it is the power of your focused and organised intellectual thoughts that will get you closer to your dream in a shorter time. Depending on your position or positioning in your life, your dreams will be weighted. This is why things do not pop up from thought straight away, there is a weight attached to them based on everything explained prior. Concerted effort, positioning, and repetitive themes of thought will polarise your dreams transforming them into goals, and then to actualisation.

INTEGRITY IS THE RIGHT ENERGY

I'm a believer in balance, measures of opposites, karmic energy, rewards and debts. I'm sure there is a little man somewhere in a room, auditing your every thought and action, which is then given to an auditor who determines the value of these minutes and what dynamism should be thrown into your life for the purposes of growth and learning. My advice to you in order to get on the auditor's side and to get the best quality minutes written of you, is to live a life of integrity. Living with integrity means being honest with people and yourself. Own up to situations where you were wrong, and find ways to rectify them. When you are honest, you are letting go of any latent negative potential from building up inside you. People will respect you for your honesty, and you are much more valued compared to a person who tries to lie their way into people's hearts only because they care about temporary opinions. If you cannot do something, let someone know in advance, it is not fair on them and yourself to pretend to have the capacity or skill to do something. If you're not sure if you can complete a task, let the person know that it is unlikely to be done, however bear in mind that you shall give it your best shot, that way you are giving yourself leniency. If you know that you feel certain you can complete a task, give people the surety they need in order to trust in your abilities. There is a balance, as you cannot continuously say you can do things, and shouldn't continuously say you can't do things out of caution and fear. Be honest, but don't be afraid to push yourself. Integrity is also sticking to morals and principles that define you as a person. Make sure that you stick to your principles, don't be loose by any means. If you say you are going to do something, make sure you do it. Become a person who does what they say. Be a person who is not afraid to stand up for what is right. Be a person who is courteous and respectful to their fellow human. Be a person who is empathetic and considerate. Be a person who is a servant leader, and develops mutualistic benefits and opportunities. Stick with these principles and you'll be a bundle of integrity. Integrity is also about being holistic and well rounded. Observe and manage carefully the areas in your life, and determine how best you can enhance them. Remember, some areas may need more attention than others, but this is what balance is. There is no way you can give the same level of attention to finance as you do to your spiritual life, you need to assess how much effort is deserved for that specific area and appropriately take the right action towards it; this is balance and living a life with integrity.

CHAPTER FOUR

TENACITY

ABOVE AND BEYOND IS A PLACE FOR WINNERS

There are no secrets to success. It is the result of preparation, hard work and learning from failure.

Collin Powell

POSITION YOURSELF FOR SUCCESS

Being at the right place, at the right time, with the right skill, and the right people around you is what is defined as positioning. It is manifesting the right situation from the get go by developing these areas. Positioning is an art, and it is developed by those who see themselves as visionaries, in other words, the people in our lives who can see beyond the Now. Be constantly aware of what it is you need to achieve in order to perform in the right position. Let's say you weren't in the right place, but the timing was right, and you had the skill, and the right people around you, you may be unqualified for success, or gain a new learning opportunity. What if you had all the factors except for timing? Again, a learning opportunity would be exercised. However, learning from these experiences is still a form of positioning, because it flags what is missing, and what you must do in order to prevent this occurrence from happening again. I call this Progressive Positioning. If you use *Progressive Positioning* to help you climb the ladder of knowing what you need and how you must get it, eventually you will be positioned, and suitable for a successful (desired) result.

SUCCESS REQUIRES YOU TO BE HARDWORKING AND SMART

Would you rather be in a situation where you work smart or work hard? I'd probably want to work smart; it sounds great doesn't it? However, I'm just wondering what that actually means. I guess in essence it probably means working efficiently and effectively. To have lean process, you must reduce delays, defects, waiting, money, time and other factors. So that you can work lean, it means there must be a process before this that enables a person to work smart. There must have been some activity before you get to the smart stage surely? If that is the case, you would need to practice or learn the required skills or knowledge for correct execution. Being smart seems like initially it involves hard work. Let's break it down a little further, working hard is the quality of effort, consistency and persistence that you give towards something. You can almost see it synonymous to the quality of momentum one has during and after their endeavours. When we think about working smart, it is the level of specificity, focus and organisation you have towards creating a quality product or service through intelligent and effective efficiency. Combine the two and you have heaven. This is the aim ladies and gentlemen, working smart is not only smart work, it's hard work too. *Understand Reach Expand* gives you practical techniques and insights in order to develop and activate the hardworking part of the brain. In sequential books they will give you techniques to develop and activate the smart areas of the brain, so you can get the best outcomes.

THERE IS NO SECRET TO SUCCESS

When it comes down to it, you just need to do it. That's it. I could easily just end the book here, but there is no value in that. You have to tell yourself "I want my success, and I'm going to get it!" I'm telling you right now there is no secret! The word secret, especially in this industry of self-development, is used to entice lazy people to action, it is used to attract people who think formulaically and it is used for people who need hope. I'd rather say there is no secret, however there are habits, patterns, themes, processes and journeys you must endure in order to reach success. Getting to the point of your goals is hard work, there is no lying about it. But it's about lightening the load in order to manifest the workings towards your goals. If you can accept that there is hard work involved, then most of you will get where you want to and success will be closer than you think. There are no other ways, no shortcuts, no secrets, no backdoor routes, none whatsoever! However, there is plenty of pain, challenges, tears, stress, and frustration. Before you get delusional over what you are reading, please remember there is no gain, without pain. Pain is necessary, it is part of the school of life. If you know that life is a school, and it is simply a learning experience, then it becomes easier, the only condition is you decide how you want to graduate in life.

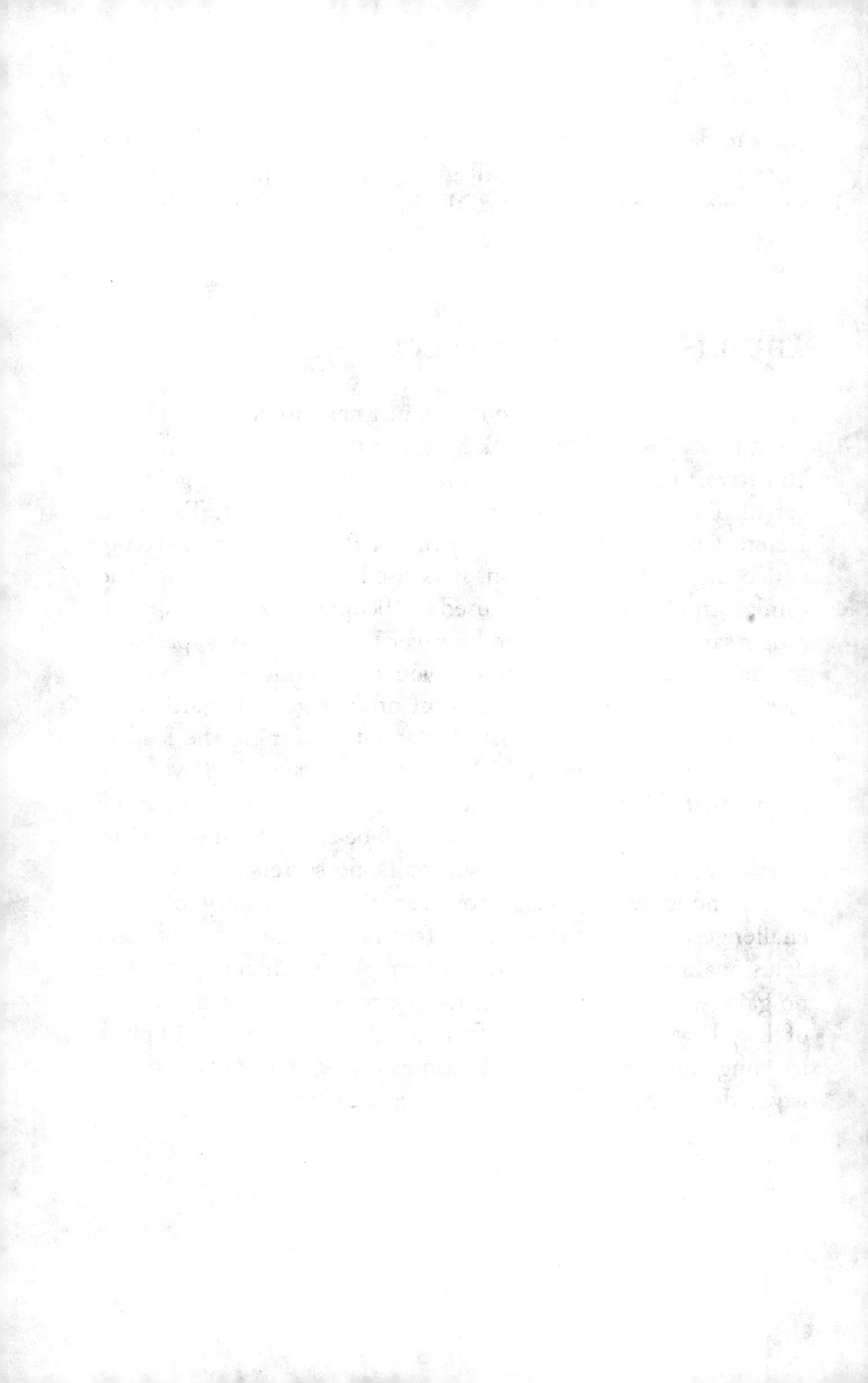

CHAPTER FIVE

NEEDS

DEFINING NEEDS AND WANTS

*Doing what needs to be done may not make you happy,
but it will make you great.*

George Bernard Shaw

A NEED IS SOMETHING NECESSARY FOR SURVIVAL

Our needs are necessary to continue a process. We need oxygen to support our respiratory functions; we need water and food to maintain biochemical and physiological processes in our body; we need shelter to protect us from wear and tear from our environment; we need to urinate and excrete to prevent poisoning from ourselves; and we need people around us to starve loneliness inside and establish connections and value. We can't avoid these things because we have indicators that reminds us of our needs. The human body was designed to input, process, and output information, so charmingly that it can finely control the output, delaying or accelerating an outcome, or varying the measure of quality that is produced from it. Using our human body as an example, think about what is needed from you in order to support your dreams. What skills, capabilities, and actions are needed for you to perform? Keep a list of what you think you need to perform at the level you need too. This list must be scrutinised. It must be a list that includes what is vital for the transition from where you are, to where you want to be.

A WANT IS DESIRED

Wants are the sprinkles and cream to everyone's cake, they are the interior leather in a person's car, and they are the first class modes of transport in our society. What we want is not needed, it is desired and therefore is a strong feeling of wishing for something to happen. Why? If you haven't realised this already we are all chasing feeling, a desired or preferred state of feeling that gives us a perceived experience. It is reciprocal in nature. Some of us want a constant state of these feelings, generated from circumstances that arise, others want this feeling at an instant. The relative distance of experience towards our feelings cause either pain or pleasure, i.e. physical or mental stress or enjoyment and satisfaction. It could be argued that wants create enhanced value in your life. You need a collection of temporary and long term wants to satisfy our human possessive nature. We must also remember not to be overly consumed and overcome by our wants, unless it is directed towards your long term vision and goal, where it is positive, progressive, and holds value for you and others without putting others at deliberate or intentional harm. This is why it's important to write down all your wants, it sets the standards for your life, it gives you purpose and direction no matter how superficial things may seem to others. I believe that we must all have at least one main want in life that will make you feel proud once obtained, but I also believe in little wants, wants that'll build an area in your life.

Here are some examples of primary motivating factors that

people have, adopted from the book *Questions are the Answers*, *Allan Pease*:

- Extra Income

- Financial Freedom

- Own a business

- More spare time

- Personal Development

- Helping others

- Meeting new people

- Retirement

- Leave a legacy

Whatever your primary motivating factor is in life, follow the steps in book one and go out and get it. It is your life, one that is loaned to us in a physical body via infinite energetic intelligence, use it don't abuse it.

TRANSFORM YOUR WANTS INTO NEEDS AND BECOME POWERFUL

There are clearly some wants that people have that feel like they are too powerful to just let go. If anything they have become a need because you have attached a compelling reason towards them that gives you a futuristic preferred state of your life. Here are some steps to transform your strong burning wants into needs.

1. State and write down the want

2. State why you want it so badly

3. State what it will add to your life

4. Is your want going to be progressive or regressive in an area of your life?

5. State how it will make you feel

6. State how it will make you feel if you don't achieve it in the next 30-90 days, or 6-12 months

7. Write down what is needed to get this want

8. How much money is required for this want? Do you have enough currently? If not how can you get more?

9. Does your 'want' impact any area of your life negatively?

10. Why is this your priority want over all other wants?

Some of these questions reinforce each other. If you really want it, you'll go out and get it regardless. This exercise simply confirms and also strengthens your desire, consolidates what you want and gives you sufficient fire in your belly to go out and do it. You can choose to do this exercise by yourself, or with someone you trust, however do not wait on them, get it done.

CHAPTER SIX

FOCUS

CUT OUT THE CRAP AND FOCUS

Focus is a matter of deciding what things you're not going to do.

John Carmack

CREATE A PRIORITY MATRIX

Follow one course until successful, I promise you there is no other way. You must be in a position to learn how to become a master of one trade and definitely not a jack of all. There is a way to stand out from the rest, however you need to excel prolifically at a specific skill in order to show red in the large patch of green. One great thing you can do is to use a priority matrix to determine what is high on your priorities and what isn't. The ability to act on priorities is what makes someone a somebody. Develop the skill of identifying:

1. What needs to be done at the earliest opportunity?

2.   What smallest act will give the biggest impact?

3.   What is important?

4.   What is urgent?

Use the following figure to help you decide your priorities.

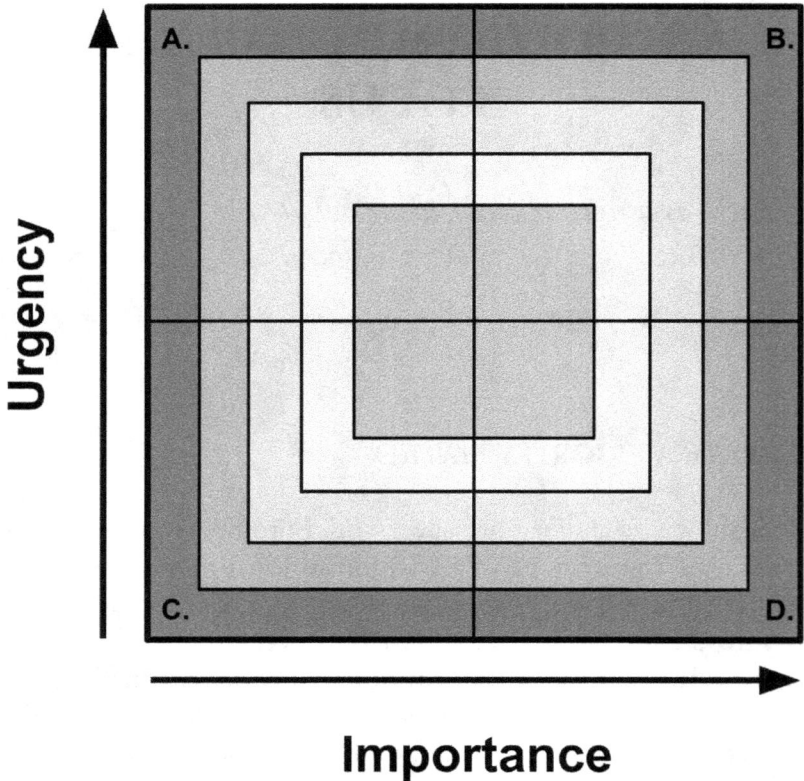

FOCUS ON YOUR PRIORITIES

Now that you have decided your priorities using the priorities matrix, look at what you have prioritised, and focus on getting it done. The idea is to think about how, and what you intend to do in order to complete the task without too much strenuous and conscious effort, but more creative and relaxed effort. The aim is speed of implementation, i.e. as soon as it comes to you and you have given it a priority rating, get it done as soon as possible! Have you ever observed what people do when considering a goal? They overthink and over plan their actions in order to think about getting started, but don't actually start. Please do not confuse what I am saying as do not plan or strategise at all, I am merely pointing out behaviours that some people adopt as an avoidance strategy. Activity is productive when a result is obtained. Once you've decided and written down your priority just do it! There are people who benefit from this more than others. I am wired to act on impulse and get things done as soon as possible, because I know that if I delay I'm less inclined to do it. I have also realised that overtime my interest levels decline and I look for the next project to quickly complete. Why am I saying this? Because It's good to know how you respond to work, and how managing your behaviours will carry you towards the finish line. One of my friends is more wired towards a "slow and very steady wins the race" sort of mentality, but he adds on things to create a more acute picture, which in effect could potentially slow him down. What would benefit him is writing down his priorities and following through with one assured plan regardless of what other possible plans there are. Variation of ideas and plans are good, but you have to make a decision through the planning process, and once that has been completed, leave planning to one side and start executing. Let's be clear here planning is usually a sequential and logical tick-list or action log of things to do, it's nothing fancy. When you incorporate your reviewing stage, then you can tweak your plans if necessary. Focus on what you must complete, and do it with speed of implementation.

POSITIONING ALLOWS YOU TO FOCUS

I'm actually saying this out loud as I type: "I absolutely love the concept of positioning!" It gives me a quantitative feel about how I think success works not only for myself, but for others who have achieved it or on the road to it. It is very simple to understand. Positioning explained simply goes as follows: Positioning yourself is doing the right thing, at the right time, with the right people, in the right place. If there is anything, absolutely anything that you pick up from this book it is that statement: doing the right thing, at the right time, with the right people, in the right place. When you have this at the forefront of your mind then success becomes easier to imagine, and therefore plan and take action on. Ask yourself these questions:

- Am I doing the right things to achieve my sole goal?

- Am I on track with my goal?

- Am I communicating with the right considered experts supporting different parts of my goal?

- Am I in the right environments that will impact me getting closer to my goals in a positive and progressive manner?

Ask yourself these questions daily, and come up with answers that tailors and steers you towards taking the right sort of quality action. Oprah Winfrey describes what she think's luck is, and pretty much this will sum up this topic and the concept of positioning:

"I believe luck is preparation meeting opportunity. If you hadn't prepared when the opportunity came along, you wouldn't have been lucky"

If you can position yourself and better yet get people to position you more effectively, success will be knocking on your door. It doesn't have to be done yourself, after all the wise get others to aid and enhance their position for success.

☆ Daily Goal Provoking Questions ☆

Am I doing the right things to achieve my goal?

Am I on track with my goal?

Am I communicating with the right considered experts supporting different parts to my goal?

Am I in the right environments that will impact me getting closer to my goals in a positive and progressive manner?

CHAPTER SEVEN

CONCENTRATION

THE TECHNIQUES THAT BIRTH CONCENTRATION

Concentration and mental toughness are the margins of victory.

Bill Russell

CATEGORISE THE PEOPLE IN YOUR LIFE

This sounds overly pedantic but it is an extremely useful tool for organising your phone book directory, and essentially the people in your life. The way that most people know how to do this is via their phones. Before you add someone to your phone book do the following, check to see whether your phone can place people into categories, if so here are some ideas of categories that you may want to use: *my circle, family, religious community, business, education, exercise and sport, Don't pick up and work.* If you can think of more or even less categories that are relevant to you, by all means use those categories. What is the importance of doing this? It allows you to very clearly see who is in your life and the area of life that they support you in. If multiple people support multiple areas, add them to those categories. I use Google contacts to categorise people in my phone book, making it easier to update and transfer onto other mobile devices. I never get rid of telephone numbers, as you never know when someone may positively come back into your life. Saying that, I'd also like to know if any psychos are trying to re-enter my life. It pays to know who you are communicating with. Use your phone directory to the maximum and fill out the notes section, mention where you met them, enter any additional forms of information that you have of them, like their address, email, work number, birthday etc. The more you know and have on a person, the better you can relate to them, and essentially create more perceived value in their life. If you have a conversation about someone, and they reveal something profound or new to you, don't feel shy about adding this information to your contacts notes section. This is important because it allows you to create relationships faster and longer because you have reminders and prompts about a person. You don't have to complete this in a day, or do your entire phone, but begin making a new habit when you meet someone, and complete their information appropriately. I know some people at networking events that take a picture of the person they have met, and upload it on their contact's picture profile, so they know what the person looks like. What a great idea! If the person is comfortable with this fire away, if not a more cautious approach that I use is to ask for their Facebook add (or other social media platform), that way you know what they look like and you can also track their social media lifestyle. Get into the habit of categorising, and relationships will be easier to build.

AFFORD AN ACCOUNTABLE OFFICER

Having someone by your side through thick and thin is a smart tactic to adopt when trying to succeed in an endeavour. Think about this carefully, there are two types of people, people who would rather be alone, and people who would rather be around people. Furthermore, people need people for growth, insight and opportunity. The measure of compatibility and personal power a person has over another will determine how cohesive they are. Bearing this in mind you can pair up or buddy up with a person to make them your accountability officer. This person would be the one you report to in order to explain and justify your actions and decisions, and give them the power of feedback that is aligned to your goals. Your officer must be aware, be clear with, understand your vision and what you aim to realise in order to effectively work with you. This person must possess leadership qualities such as the ability to communicate effectively (listening and speaking), be honest and genuine, have an objective and due diligent approach, and be invested in your best interests. How can you find someone who is invested in your best interests? Unless they are a family member that respects and loves you dearly, or a friend that you share this commonality with that is genuine and thorough, it may be difficult to find someone. It serves well at times to have people you do not know, but you also share common goals with. This is a unique opportunity because the person doesn't feel obliged to have to lie to you, if anything they are more likely to want to feedback useful information to you because it is learning for them, in addition, potentially healthy competition. You can find people like this at networking events, seminars, and events dedicated to accountability partnership. If you want to speed up on your dreams, find an accountability partner.

BE CLEAR OF YOUR VISION

Your vision is the light in the sky, it is the beam you are chasing in order to satisfy your very existence. It pays to know your vision very well, and be in a state where you are living your vision. Have your vision written on a piece of paper, or inside your journal that clearly defines what you want to achieve, what you see in your vision and briefly how you will achieve it. Your vision should trigger thought and feeling, emotion that excites you in the present state, and gets you feeling a little uneasy that you haven't got to the end goal yet. Is there ever an end? No, however conquering one mountain shows your real human potential. If your vision changes or adapts, it means that you cannot make up your mind of what you truly want. On the other hand you could be getting good at achieving your original goal, making your vision clearer and more refined. A lot of us learn by speaking to people about what we know, so be in a position to talk about your vision to people. Be in a position where you can excite people about your vision. In my following books, there are SMART techniques that can help you plan out what you must do to get closer and closer to the beam of light. Without sight you are nothing, and sight comes from belief in what you want, and knowing what you want well. Many people do not know what they want, therefore they do not look for what they want because it doesn't exist to them. Everybody came into this world eventually wanting something, big or small depending upon perspectives, however there is an underlying want that really falls under overlapping themes. Maslow attempts to talk about our human needs, and as you climb higher up the hierarchy these 'basic needs' are shaped by experience formed from conditions, circumstances and consequences, that form our perspectives, shaped by our economic, social, political and cultural environments that feed into what we want. Or is this wrong? Were we born knowing

what we want, after all what defines us as being born?
Regardless of the actual root of our internal desires we have
wants, and we have the ability to satisfy them by creating goals
to achieving our vision. Be the vision!

CHAPTER EIGHT

PURPOSE

DESIRE IS THE DRIVER BEHIND PURPOSE

Figure out who you are, then do it on purpose.

Dolly Parton

DESIRE HELPS YOU REALISE YOUR PURPOSE

Desire is something you can't automatically have, it comes upon you like a male lion primed and ready to pounce upon its mate. The deep intense feeling of wanting something will move you to go and do something about it. How is that this overwhelming feeling is generated in the first place? When you are fixated on an experience that makes you think and therefore feel a certain way, which puts you in a state of mind, you either don't want to experience that feeling again or you want to feel it more regularly. An experience reveals to you through feeling a series of thoughts and ideas, the theme of your thinking, and therefore powerfully governs your attitudes. Desire can only be achieved through a firm want for something derived out of an experience. Think about the situations you don't want to be in, and why it means so much for you not to be in those situations again. Are you willing to do what it takes? Resilience on autopilot is needed, you cannot let things like tiredness and light hunger get in the way of the tasks you must embark upon in order to tick tasks off your desire list.

DESIRE DEFINES CLARITY OF ACTION

The reason(s) 'why' supports your burning desire to win and gives you the right foundation for your actions. Because your reason is personal and in relation to your experiences or visionary needs, it gives you that extra drive to get started and keep on going. A desire to succeed is key but that desire needs to be purchased with a commitment to understand how you plan to achieve your goal. Knowing your reason behind your internal desires gives you energy, purpose and the motivation to act. As a plan and a strategy gives you the stepping stones and positioning for action, they can also direct you towards your desire. This means there are two waves of understanding stemmed from self-belief and from the structure you get from planning. Action derives from both of these waves of understanding because the reasons for your desires are internalised and expressed through feeling, and can be channelled and refined via a proven plan. This creates a drive for taking targeted action. On the flip side your current actions will reveal what desires are dominant in your life. If you are in a position where you don't know what you want and therefore feel no sense of desire for achievement, go back to my first book *Understand Reach Expand: 15 Super Effective ways to Manage your Mind*, and complete the exercises to create a sense of desire and want. You have to have an attitude of certainty locked into your mind that is uncompromising to the needs of matching or obtaining your desires.

Desire Enables Meaning Behind Motives

What we do repeatedly is a result of our accumulated thoughts. Have you ever thought why you do what you do? Have you ever thought why you are doing the job you are doing, or why you are studying the course you are studying? Have you ever thought why you are with the partner you are with? Think back to the original feeling and modes of thinking. We usually do things to obtain value in our lives, or avoid pain in our lives. What were you avoiding? What were you trying to gain? Did your plan work and if so what were the results? There are many people in jobs for the purposes of just paying their bills. Other people are in jobs for experience sake in order to boost their prospects for other opportunities. Without going back to the real reason as to why they are interested in their job, they may wander into it with a dissatisfying taste, just tolerating the position because too much has happened to change course now, they are too old, or have a family to look after. There are also people in jobs that want to climb the career ladder just because they can. This may be to boost their egos and develop a sense of identity, maybe even to develop power, prestige or financial opportunities. But the responsibility that builds up from these egotistical desires does not seem attractive to the majority in the long-run, so again they are stuck. Why would you go through all of this and still not be happy? Because you cannot predict the future with no desire, even still you do not control the course of your future without the finesse of knowing what you truly want; it always boils down to this. Some people say it is hard to know what you want but really you need to talk to many people, visit multiple events and places, have an open mind and explore things in order to have an idea of your interests. You'll never know what you like and don't like, what you can tolerate and what you won't tolerate if you do not expose yourself to varied environments. Your motives will be flawed and go against the intrinsic feeling of what your true purpose and desires are here on earth.

CHAPTER NINE

WILLPOWER

THE DIFFERENCES BETWEEN STRENGTH AND WILLPOWER

Power over a man's subsistence is power over his will.

Alexander Hamilton

LEARN TO PERFORM LONG AFTER THE FEELING IS GONE

When talking about strength I am referring to most people's understanding of willpower; essentially I'm talking about power. In physics Power is the Force applied to an object over a specific distance per unit of time, as can be seen in the diagram below. It can also be described as the Work Done by an object, per unit time.

$$\frac{(Force \ x \ distance)}{Time}$$

Or

$$\frac{\underline{Work\ Done}}{Time}$$

What does this mean? Well, Force is Mass multiplied by Acceleration, i.e. the rate at which an object moves through space, and the distance signifies the length that the object moves through space. So we are saying that Power is the rate at which an object moves to a specific destination. How does this translate into your life? Well essentially, you (the Mass) applied to the quality of your work ethic and action towards your goal, attached to a deadline, per hour, determines your willpower, or mental strength and quality of action. Power is your ability to get yourself to take effective action in order to achieve a result in a given amount of time; this is how you should think of willpower from now on. Move yourself to take action and decide you will reach your goals in a given amount of time.

MAINTAIN QUALITY THROUGHOUT

If you look at the definition of strength on Google it is *the quality or state of being physically strong*, and if you look up the definition of strong it is *having the power to move heavy weights or perform physically demanding tasks, in addition to, able to withstand force, pressure, or wear*. I think this amazingly describes the qualities we must have in order to be successful and get to a point of achievement. Strength is a quality that someone has that warrants them to perform to a standard that makes them believe what they want to achieve. Strength comes from the quality of knowing what you want, and practicing, grafting, and doing what it takes to get it. Strength is also the quality of passing through barriers, and not being inhibited by potential barriers. If the quality (the standard of measure against other practices, or the degree of variation from a mean) improves, then your potential for success is more likely to be realised. I find it interesting that you can measure yourself against a degree of excellence, surely you must have an example of what that excellence looks like before you define that quality? Make sure you discover what excellence looks like, so you can understand what excellence is. That way you are more than likely to get closer to your aim.

CONTROL YOUR EMOTIONAL STATE THROUGHOUT

Quality, strength, and willpower is fundamentally swayed by your emotional intelligence. It is governed by your ability to control your emotional state that serves your goal. Irrational and sometimes uncalculated actions can lead to the end of your life, it is better to be aware of how you act in situations and find ways to adapt your response to them appropriately. It is suggested that you learn, observe and analyse human behaviours in your environment, and monitor how they respond to your responses. Rather than focusing on how you feel based on a response someone gives you, focus more on why you think they gave you a particular response, aiming to see it from their point of view. This is best done from an objective or an empathetic point of view. Once you have seen it from their point of view, ask yourself is there something you want to manage and adapt with how you respond, or do you want to continue to react a particular way emotionally? Remember emotions are not all bad, it is just an expression of your internal and usually primitive self. They can be controlled but do not always have to be, sometimes you can let leash depending on the situation.

In specific situations or after an event, you could also ask friends or family members why they think you responded to situations the way you did, It'll be interesting and good learning to see who actually is aligned with your mode of thinking, and it will show you how observant they are, and potentially how clued up they are as well. Make sure to note the new things that are revealed to you, as this in itself may be enough for you to change your emotional state(s) for the better. If you are a person who does not like to be constructively criticised, then this may be difficult for you. Learn to listen and record what people say about you; this is how we learn and grow. Whether you think they are right or wrong, for now it doesn't matter. What is more important is knowing why they made particular observations, digesting their reasoning and concluding whether their reasoning follows a reasonable logic. Before you finish this subtopic, look up the definition of emotional intelligence on Google, and you will find the instructions to what you must do in order to become an emotionally intelligent individual. Essentially emotional intelligence focuses on self-awareness, controlling your responses, social awareness, and managing relationships. For a deeper understanding on this topic, check out the book Emotional Intelligence, By Daniel Goleman.

CHAPTER TEN

WINNING

DEVELOP A WINNING ATTITUDE

Winners never quit and quitters never win.

Vince Lombardi

KNOW WHAT YOU WANT TO WIN

Don't you think it is fair to say that a competition is usually won when you know you are competing, and you are aware of what you could win as first prize? Some people enter life not knowing what prize they want, let alone being in any competition. People don't even know that they are partaking in life's competition. The competition involves finding your purpose or primary aim in life as accurately as possible, and aligning yourself to it. The accuracy for finding your primary aim is dependent on how much it resonates with you, and the measure of desire it invokes into your heart. It must activate a "no matter what" kind of attitude in order to compel you to act with purpose and passion. It has been shown by Dr Melissa

Cardon, Professor of Management at Lubin School of Business at Pace University, that passion is key to realising an entrepreneurial endeavour, or any endeavour for that matter, so it is important to align yourself to something that you are passionate about pursuing. The end goal is more important than the means goal, i.e. know your ultimate reason why you are doing something as opposed to the distractions of mini hopes and dreams. It doesn't need to be complicated it just needs to be a truth that connects to your emotional centres. Athletics is a great example of this as it enlightens the imagination of this point. The greatest athletes in the world know their aims and targets, and they train, diet, and live a lifestyle that tailors towards it. Before they knew their greatness they were inspired or encouraged by someone else to compete. Let's reflect upon your life, what is your competition? What is the prize that you are after? What are you prepared to do in order to win your prize? You need to be uncompromising and have a relentless attitude towards what you want to achieve. Look, let's be very clear, people want to win, so why should you have to compromise? A winning attitude is developed by taking what you want extremely seriously, and taking mass imperfect action with the utmost zeal. Put your dream first in a way that maintains integrity, respect, and puts yourself in situations that provide a win-win for you and others. It doesn't make sense to just win for yourself, help others win too. In actual fact, that is how you win faster! Who is involved in the winning process when a football team wins a competition,? The strikers, midfielders, defenders, the goal-keepers, the subs and reserves, the coaches, the physios, the football clubs associations and the fans; the fans even say "We won!" but did they actually play the game? No, however they were part of the winning experience. To summarise, a winning attitude allows you to:

- Know your competition

- Know what the prize is

- Activate your desire to win

- Discover what you're willing to do to get first prize

- Recognise who will win with you

- Help others win competitions along the way

To finalise, know where you are, and where you need to be, the rest will work itself out with enough passion, enthusiasm, and desire.

DEVELOP YOUR STRENGTHS

You need strength. Let me repeat this, you need strength. When you have this quality in its true form you are really saying, "I don't care what anyone says I am going to do this no matter what it takes". It is bashing through barriers with hunger in order to get to your goal. Strength is what encapsulates the weight of which you are willing to carry on the journey. The weight refers to suffering, experiences, people, environments, conditions, circumstances and consequences. The best way to develop strength is to experience what it is you fear and endure it. The first way you do this is through acknowledging your strengths from the beginning, and getting others to do the same for you too. Once you do this write down a statement that acknowledges your strengths such as:

"I **am** Michael Tabirade and I **am** *perceptive*, great at managing behaviours, and *conducive*. I **am** pretty good at helping people realise their dream, in addition to **being** very *analytical* and *methodical,* whilst **being** *empathetic"*

I made the verb "am" and it's associated words bold. "Am" comes from the root word "being", which means *the nature or essence of a person, or simply to exist.* So by saying these words you are projecting existence into it. I have underlined describing words that are positive and enhancing by nature. This is to remind you how good you are at these qualities so it is important to include them. Additionally, I have also italicised any adjectives highlighted as strengths.

Once you have done this, ponder over it, adapt it if you feel necessary, and more importantly proclaim it to others at work, project environments or even in conversation. You'll begin to believe more and more that these are your strengths, and you'll begin to subconsciously do more things to notice them.

To make it clearer here is what you do to develop your strengths:

Acknowledgement is the first step.

Experience and perform these strengths to prove to others and yourself that you can do these things, and do these things well. Check your curriculum vitae (CV) and supporting statements and see if these qualities pop up. A recruiting officer once told me that some of their clients updated their CVs bi-weekly, specifically updating their strengths! Now they are on a different level to most people, however it shows that there are people out there who are up-to-date with their skill set and qualitative strengths, allowing them to propel forward in life; awareness is key.

Improvement is the final step.

You must also find ways to improve your strengths. What is available out there that enables you to become a master analyst, or an excellent facilitator? It is easy to find things to help you, but to commit to a system, structure or method is a whole different story. Find a class or a book that empowers your strengths, and gives you a platform to become incredibly effective at executing those qualities. Regularly rate your level of skill and competence and find ways to improve them. The simplest way to improve on any skill is to do the following:

1.   Gain more experience using that skill

2.   Write and reflect on your lessons learned at the end of your experiences

When you get into the habit of doing this, improvements occur because you are aware of what needs to improve, allowing you to tailor your actions towards making those improvements. For additional help on how to find your strengths, refer back to book one, Understand Reach and Expand.

ACKNOWLEDGE BUT DON'T FOCUS ON YOUR COMPETITORS

It is important to recognise who your competition is. The word competition defines an event where someone or something is trying to overcome barriers or achieve a desired result in order to stand victorious. Therefore, you must identify what's in your way, and what you are trying to overcome, in addition to, what you are aiming to achieve. Can you see that these are two sides of the same coin? One side focuses on overcoming barriers, the other side focuses on achievement. You are more than likely creating the barriers. By saying "Johnny is better than me at playing football" or "Sandra is much smarter than me" is not helpful. Are these statements really true and in what context? They may be, and if they are, accept them for what they are and move on; focus on where your strengths lie. In the book Man's Search for Meaning, Viktor E. Frankl said:

"Between stimulus and response, there is a space. In that space is our power to choose our response. In our response lies our growth and our freedom."

This means that we should focus on the control we have over our situations through our responses, we cannot always help what happens, but our response is the true determinant of our course in life. Know and understand your competition, your barriers, your setbacks, and your aims, and focus on making sure you shall overcome them and win. Sometimes our competition isn't as great as it seems and we grant it this greatness which is a huge inhibitor. You should have a certain level of arrogance, or better described as a quiet confidence, in your ability to perform to a high standard, where this should come via practicing and mastering the skills of your trade as often as possible. The knowledge through research, action and experience will build that confidence to the point where you know you have no competition. In essence, you realise the true competition has always been yourself. Get to the stage where you have no competition and do everything in your right and power to make this a reality. You've got what it takes!

CHAPTER ELEVEN

REALISM

BEING REALISTIC HAS ITS PROBLEMS

Realism is a bad word. In a sense everything is realistic. I see no line between the imaginary and the real

Federico Fellini

YOUR SENSE OF REALISM COULD BE PESSIMISM

What does being realistic mean to you? Forget what the definition actually is. For many, being realistic has become a reason for avoiding any risk due to fear of failure. Isn't being realistic representing your state of perceptive reality and your measure of thinking against a mean or comparator? Many would agree that realism can be based on empiricism but many use empirical arguments that support a higher degree of failure relative to success, when empirical measures may not always be the best way to measure a failure. We are wired to survive and not to fail; the very nature of survival is success. Barack Obama once said *"You can't let your failures define you. You have to let your failures teach you."* People let failures or the idea of failure define them or the situation they are in, therefore they become "realistic", and really are becoming pessimistic i.e. seeing the worst in a situation under the skin and makeup of a "normal thinking human being". Genuine realism is good in the context of your targets, there is no room for pessimism for your goals. Observe what appears to be realistic, and learn to measure the apparent risk against it. If you have studied and aimed to master your field, then there are no risks, only calculated actions and potential lessons you can learn from. Risk is context based, and there is always room for improvement.

YOUR SENSE OF REALISM COULD BE EXCUSES

Excuses will kill you one day if you don't stop using them. Do you think excuses are necessary? This is a very serious question? Excuses aren't necessarily a bad thing, it's just that most of the time (if not all the time) expressing an excuse is not required at all even if it appears relevant. Based on observation people use excuses as a form of justification for one's actions to reduce any form of blame or judgement that potentially could be placed upon them. People want to protect their self-image, potential reputation and ego by utilising the licence of an excuse. Some people do not care why you have not completed a task, even if it seems like a valid reason, they just want it done. I challenge you to not make a single excuse for 14 days. Just accept whatever it is you are facing and aim to take action.

Another problem with excuses is that they are seen as a form of what is realistic to a person, as they see it as an escape route; a way to avoid responsibility. How are you possibly going to get from point A to point B, and then from point B to point

C? You must be in a state of a great burning desire to climb your mountain. This is the only way you can get around excuses because you will not let small things or even big things hold you back. By having a burning desire you can see what you want and create a path in order to grab it. Excuses are usually for the weak in the context of what you are trying to achieve. There are people who have suffered heartache and pain, yet they use this heartache and pain that has happened in their life as fuel to attack their goals. Not everyone is wired this way but it starts by developing habits, and you must learn to not make excuses. Every time you are about to make an excuse, stop yourself, think about it and go on about your life. Get rid of the excuses, and the challenges will turn into learning opportunities.

ALL IDEAS WERE IMAGINED BEFORE BEING REAL

Do you want to know what I think is truly amazing? Everything around us was once invisible. A contribution of thought and then imagination that fostered the actualisation of the by-products you see today, whether that is you and I, the book or mobile device you are using, was once invisible. Here's the definition of Imagination: *the faculty or action of forming new ideas, or images or concepts of external objects not present to the senses.* You won't appreciate this definition until you break down the words within it. To have a faculty is to have an independent existing mind, or to have physical powers, one that can actively produce new thoughts and suggestions as a possible course of action. The imagination allows you to form original pictures that live in your mind's abode, yet they do not exist via your external senses, but only through the independent physical powers of consciousness and thought. Yet imagination can have a potent effect on how we sense our reality. People must be in a process of enhancing and fostering their imaginative thoughts, and activating the sections in their brain that develops their imagination. Thought impulses repeated from looking at pictures creates heightened subconscious activity wiring the universe (or you) to conspire towards these thoughts, whereby they are expressed as actions, and eventually actualisations. These were all propagated by the power of imagination. This also assumes that your emotional intent is polarised towards what these images trigger consciously for you in your mind. The researcher Alex Schlegel, part of Dartmouth College Department of Psychology and Brain sciences, has been trying to understand what part of the brain is responsible for imagination generation. fMRI scans revealed that when subjects were imagining abstract objects, and then creating complex ones from these objects, several parts of the brain were activated. Alex Schlegel states that this is part of a widespread network of neurons called the mental workspace. Studies have even shown that when athletes imagine running a race, they activate parts of the brain that contribute to movement of those muscles as if they were actually running. Imagination is an active process, where the brain uses energy and creativity to produce imaginative images and thoughts. Use mental and physical imagery from your vision boards to spark the part of the brain that activates the urge to want to start something original and unique, something that creates a smaller gap between you and your desires. There is a theory that the ether i.e. the space between things, is a soup of "ether units" that carries thought energy and intelligence, connecting all intelligent objects and beings through an integral network. This would explain the list of 20th century multiple discoveries that have been noticed throughout history around the same time; check them online. Use your imagination to develop acuity and power to act behind your creative thoughts!

CHAPTER TWELVE

HUNGER

YOU ARE RESOURCEFUL WHEN YOU ARE HUNGRY

Concentration comes out of a combination of confidence and hunger.

Arnold Palmer

FIND FOOD

We all need food to stay alive, and without it after 21 - 40 days you would die from starvation, it goes to show how durable our physical bodies actually are. We want to survive and many of us fear death. So instinctively we find food, we find food to survive to prevent death. Prevention of death may not be the initial reason but it is definitely the ultimate one. During starvation the sole aim is survival. At this point we may not necessarily think about the quality of food, as long as it is edible and classified as food that can be processed to serve bodily functions. When it comes to starvation I could even assume that some may ignore their values or morals, some may agree that their cultural or religious views would be excused, why?

Because their sole focus is to survive, they are consumed by the idea of being animate and remaining in a state to experience in the physical form, because fear of the unknown is too much for them to handle. Whatever the circumstance, you will find a way to eat in order to satisfy your stomachs, and remove yourself from the signals generated as feelings of hunger. The exact same is true when you really want to be successful in desired pursuits. The different meals you want to eat are your goals, and the hunger is your burning desire to win. How hungry are you for success? Are you hungry or are you starving? At what lengths will you go to pursue your dreams? If you can position yourself to feel like you're on the verge of starvation, you have untapped a part of you that many people do not know how to tap into. Find your hunger and go get your food.

EAT GOOD QUALITY FOOD

That point at which you bite into your food is such a euphoric experience, it is a release of intense neural impulses, where emotions are flying all over the place, expressing a deep content and satisfaction. However, the quality of what you eat determines the level at which you feel these emotions. If you happen to eat a Big Mac and fries, the initial feeling maybe of satisfaction but the aftermath is usually a feeling of regret, possibly even if you were starving. Some of you maybe at a point where you are grateful for what you have and therefore you do not complain at all. The quality of your food will determine your initial state, but ultimately your end state. Ideally, the visionary knows what sort of food will make him or her happy from the beginning, and not feel guilty or disgusted after they have consumed their meal. After all a quality meal is what we are after, and if you can find food that serves your body nutritionally well, it will serve your faculties, physiology, and internal processes to ideally be fuelled to perform at a more efficient and effective level. Develop a strategy and plan to find and make food that is of good quality, or in other words, develop a plan, strategy and goal to achieve the highest quality of success you can achieve. We live in a society where we want instant gratification, the reason why people cheat is because of instant gratification, people buy fast food because it's fast, there are kindle books because people do not want to wait the next day for their book to be delivered; people want things now. Don't let the trickery of instant gratification fool you into thinking you have achieved success through feelings. Instant gratification is so powerful that it enables the imaginative faculties, or also known as the mental workspace to become hyperactive with temporary satisfaction. Think long term, and aim for quality.

MAKE SURE YOU KEEP ON EATING

Whether you see this as an unfortunate thing or a fortunate one, we have to keep on eating to survive. What is amazing about our society is that we have done a great job to find ways to continue to eat for survival, day after day. The quality of what we eat is another story but many of us have found ways to do this. Food is exchanged for money and in order for us to fund this basic need, 95% of us trade our time for money in order to survive. So food is pretty high up there on the list of needs, however some of us do not care about the quality of what we put into our mouths. Should we care? Well to be honest that is dependent on the objective a person is trying to achieve. For the sake of maintaining a healthy lifestyle let's use a simple metric of BMI and body measurements as a measure. If your BMI is between 18.5 - 24.9 (Male and Female) then it is fair to say your food does not terribly affect your weight on drastic levels, however if your blood sugar levels are high in synthetic sugars floating around, that may be affecting your internal biochemistry and physiological performance. Do you just want good food for taste? Do you believe your body's a temple? Do you simply what to eat for survival? Why do you eat? We know the basic reasons; however, we create additional reasons that serve an aim we have in life. Let's bring this back to your goals. If you know what you want in life, if you know your aims and targets, then what you put into life, is what you get out, in other words "You are what you eat". Discover the path you need to take in order to extract the best quality outcomes and outputs that snug nicely in relation to your goals.

CHAPTER THIRTEEN

ENDURANCE

WHERE DOES ENDURANCE COME FROM?

Every calamity is to be overcome by endurance.

Virgil

DEVELOP A STRONG MINDSET

We have already defined the qualities of mindset and strength, but when we combine them together we get endurance. This really describes your human capacity to outlast an activity or task, the amount of battery life you have left that contributes to your goal. The only way to maintain drive towards your goal is by understanding two things:

1. Following ONE COURSE until successful

2. Building your self-image in order to perform better

When you follow one course, you have less energy and interest in distractions. The more units of time you spend on your course, the more likely you are to be successful in it. This prevents obstacles and barriers from slowing you down, or even causing you to stop. The man or woman who knows what they must do to win a long distance race, is a man or woman who understands what it means to go through the process of success. Lifestyle, food and diet, exercise, discipline, good sleep and a vision coupled with determination and belief, is what is needed for their success. Running 26 miles is not easy but you can do very well if you have dedicated time to set yourself up to win. Time always wins and rewards the one who plays it's game.

When you create and implement strategies that will enhance your self-esteem and image, a truer version of yourself will begin to realise that life is really a big experiment, one that enables growth through experience if you allow it to. The aim of the game is to realise your potentials and actualize them through personal growth via your experiences. Develop mechanisms that you repeat avidly in order to develop your self-image. *Understand Reach Expand* will give you some ideas of what you can do.

YOUR DESIRE TO SUCCEED ALWAYS WINS

"The will to win, the desire to succeed, the urge to reach your full potential... these are the keys that will unlock the door to personal excellence"

- Confucius.

He has a point. Wanting to win has to come from wanting something, and if you don't know what you want then how can you want to succeed? If you do, what do you want to succeed in? Ask yourself how clearly you can answer these questions. If you still haven't explored some ideas as to what you want in life stop now and go back to the beginning of the book to jog your memory. Desire is a planted seed that grows exponentially into a mighty force by absorbing what you want out of life into your own. Here's a quick story for you:

A young high school boy has a major crush on Amaka in his class. He feels that he doesn't have a hope in hell when it comes to asking her out on a date. Every so often he would freakishly stare at her, and begin to utter words, but nothing would come out, and unimpressed, she would walk away. One day the boy wondered and said to himself "If I want Amaka to be my girlfriend, I need to be confident and just ask her! I'm going in". That night the boy went to sleep as a kid, and woke up as a man. He was confidently thrusting his hips as he walked, and had his chest held high, looking a bit awkward for a scrawny 14-year-old boy. He saw Amaka, walked up to her, tapped her on the shoulder, she turned around and he said "Amaka, I've been meaning to say this for a while and today is the day where I tell you, you rock my world, will you be my girlfriend?!" There was an eerie silence, the whole classed looked at him, then looked at her... 5 seconds passed and everyone was laughing except for him. She walked closer to him and whispered in his and said, "Sorry not with you". Feeling defeated he reluctantly walked to his desk. At that time the teacher just walked in to start the lesson. The teacher was confused but nonetheless imminently started the class. The boy was just thinking about a way to ask Amaka again. The day came to a close and the boy was coming back from the library. He saw Amaka in the distance, looking as if she was making her way from cheerleading practice to the bus stop. They were headed the same way. The young boy said to himself "Thank you Lord, I know this is a chance". He walked up to her and said "Hey", she looked at him and said "Hey... Sorry about what happened earlier today, being put on the spot like that in front of everyone makes me nervous". The boy replied by saying "No problem, I should have been more considerate". They jumped on the bus, and had 60 minutes of alone time to talk together. Let's just say 10 years later, Amaka and the boy got married, and were both thriving in their relationship.

The boy did not give up his mission to be with Amaka, and his initial spark of courage is the reason why he lives a great life with his beautiful wife. Know what you want, pick up the courage to go and get it, and don't stop until you win!

DEVELOP THE RIGHT HABITS

Many people are unaware of the habits they enact daily. According to the book *The Power of Habits: Why we do what we do, and how to change,* by Charles Duhigg, 40% of our decisions made are actually habits. In fact we act upon cues that end up following a routine, in order to receive a reward. This forms what is known as a "habit loop." This could also describe the concept for positioning yourself for success i.e. set yourself up in an environment where you have a greater opportunity to act upon your "success actions" in order to reward yourself with the results you need. The power behind developing the right habits is done by understanding how habits work. It is so important to make sure that you make the right decisions, because a good proportion of your decisions turn into habits, habits that create a theme and pattern in your life that leads to results, embedding beliefs about yourself and what you think you are capable of doing. When you observe how habits work and how they are linked to your brain activity, the book reveals that your old core habits are stored in the lower central parts of the brain, and "new habits" begin forming neurological pathways at the top of your brain in the grey matter. If you are able to keep these actions through a routine, you develop what is known as a habit loop, and creating a craving for yourself as you expect a reward. The more embedded a habit, the less neuroactivity is associated with it, and the more "automatic" it is. Think about it, you want to get to the stage of automation. The real secret is understanding your habits, acknowledging your cues, routines and rewards, and tweaking your routines in order to establish more rewards creating a positive feedback loop.

Write down 10 habits that you need to adopt for your chosen field, and create 4 columns:

- Habit (the habit you need to adopt)

- Environment (the setup for success)

- Method of Operation (what needs to be done frequently)

- Prize (what you will get that develops a positive feeling).

Habit	Environment	Method of Operation	Prize
Going to the gym.	Bag packed for the gym. Must go straight after work. Must start between 5:00 - 5:30 pm.	Pack gym clothes on the weekend or night before. Go to sleep early in order to finish early. Head to the gym	Feeling of being fit. Fruit Smoothie and a great meal.

This is a real life example that I have used. My friends this works! Just try it and see what it will do for you. Positioning yourself for habit adaption will be the one thing that changes your life. Make the decision, and make positive life changing habits.

CHAPTER FOURTEEN

PASSION

GIVE YOUR LIFE MEANING

Live your life with passion.

Les Brown

PASSION ALIGNS YOU TO THE UNIVERSE

I want you to think about this, there will never be another you ever again. Even in this moment of time as you are reading this, you will never get that moment again. Whether you are an identical twin, or have someone who looks like you, acts like you, or even thinks like you, you are still unique. What makes us unique are our experiences, and what we perceive from them. They can never be exactly the same as someone else's because you own them. I know this because you are the only person experiencing your experiences, and perceiving them through your version of reality. We may share common sensory capabilities picked up from a dimension and platform meant for experiencing, however it will never be the same. You have to understand how important this is no matter how small and similar we are to each other.

Two identical twins were interviewed about their upbringing, in particular it related to their rough childhood. They were both asked separately "How did your father's abusive character, and heavily alcoholic nature affect you growing up?" The first twin said "It was horrible, I couldn't stand it and it really put me down. It made me very wary of who to trust and to whom to speak to". The other twin was asked the same question and he said "It motivated me to live my life with passion and purpose, there was no way history was going to repeat itself down this life. If anything, I appreciate the environment because it wouldn't have made me the multi-millionaire that I am today." The source of your meaning in life relates to you only. Allow yourself to stand out from the crowd and know that your life is your own, only to be seen through your eyes. You are solely responsible and in charge of your ship and you direct it towards your desired destination.

PURPOSE MAKES YOU UNIQUE

Once you wholeheartedly understand that you are completely unique, it means that you can create a unique purpose because it is attached to you. You can argue that some, if not all of our ideas and pursuits, have already been done to some extent. Here we must focus on the words "...to some extent" as this signifies a difference. Therefore, this means that no matter how similar your purpose is to someone else's, you are still warranted to embark on the journey based on the fact that you are unique. If anything, you should use another person's experiences as a platform for learning in order to fortify your journey. When you get a sense of purpose merely from knowing that you are different or that there is something unique about you, it makes you want to dance like no one is in the room and run like you can run 9 seconds flat; you embellish a power that is resonating from the core of your heart that radiates into your very being. Know your sense of uniqueness and use intention to drive your experience consciously.

PURPOSE IGNITES YOUR DESIRE TO PROVE YOUR WORTH

When you understand your uniqueness, your experiences and who you have become based on what has happened in your life. This enables you to extrapolate your potential based on what you have learned in life. Your learnings from situations determine your potential for value, however your results represent a tangible image of your worthiness. Your personal life attaches meaning to your actions, therefore defines qualitative growth. When your father says "You can't do that, do something else" some people accept it or see it as an opportunity to prove their worth. When your mother says "You think you know best, you look silly now," some may accept what they say or see it as an opportunity to improve. I'm not saying that parents or other hierarchical and accountable people in your life are negative and wrong all the time, what I am saying is that what they say can impact you so much more than your average Joe. On the flip side, if your sister says "I look up to you, I believe you can do it," or you brother says "don't listen to anyone I know you're great," that is always positive encouragement and reminds you that you should at least continue for their sake. Whatever side the coin is flipped, it shows that we respond when a feeling is evoked by people we place importance on. Usually these people are able to emotionally shift our state drastically based on what they say or do. Whether it is people or experiences, both challenge us to perform to a standard that should draw out our potential. Know your uniqueness, establish the right habits, react positively to your personal life and use it as fuel to drive you.

CHAPTER FIFTEEN

SATISFACTION

SATISFACTION FULFILS AN EXPECTATION

Satisfaction lies in the effort, not in the attainment, full effort is full victory.

Mahatma Gandhi

No one can actually be satisfied

No matter how high the mountain is, or how long it took you to get to the mountain, once you have reached that hill you have a few options. You could:

1. Admire the view and stay where you are at the peak of the mountain. But to be honest you may end up getting bored doing that

2. Go down the mountain and do something else

3. Climb another mountain

The focus transitions from wanting to climb a mountain to

wanting to do something else. Really you could combine all three of these options by admiring the view at the top and eventually, out of boredom, trek down the mountain with the aim to find another one to climb. If you never attempt to climb your mountain, then climbing the mountain is one of the only things that you will think will satisfy your life. Once you get closer to the mountain you will start to feel the satisfaction created by travelling towards that mountain. When you have reached the peak of the mountain, that satisfaction will eventually reach its summit and in due course you'll want to do something else that drives you. Manage your satisfactions; the best way to do this is to enjoy and appreciate the journey. Once you have reached the peak of your mountain, make sure you capture and record the moment in all of its entirety and look at what you have done to get so far. Once the feeling of satisfaction dissipates or you feel you want more, do not disregard or ignore what you have done, if anything take time out to look at what you have achieved and what you need to do to climb your next mountain. It is all about timing and understanding when to move in order to prevent discouragement and negativity over your past failures.

SATISFICATION QUENCHES TEMPORARY DESIRES

You must aim to be a visionary and developing this art involves knowing what you want and being bold about it. You must have a big, creative imagination, you must plan effectively to strategically position yourself to act on your thoughts and ideas, and be able to motivate and inspire people around you to see your vision and do the same, regardless of how crazy it is. During the times when you are working towards your vision, you need to create goals that have a prize at the end of it no matter how small. What you are doing here is motivating yourself to act even more effectively. If you continuously put your head down and work hard, you'll wear yourself out and you'll become exhausted, in addition, you'll probably not want to aim for your vision anymore. I speak from experience and have suffered from exhaustion, having been run down for 3 weeks at a time on numerous occasions, developed repetitive strain injury and even developed cluster headaches over the course of 6 weeks. This chapter is referring to a balance you must create in order to be on course for your goal. I agree that you need to work hard, but you must give yourself rewards in order to get yourself in touch with reality. This can even come in the form of rest. As a good friend once said "reward yourself on the little things, even if it's from getting up earlier that day" the brain needs to know that you have done something good and therefore you should expect a reward. Temporary propulsions of treating yourself partnered with motivation, creates a train of habit that pulls you closer and closer to your vision.

DEVELOP A REWARD SYSTEM

This part is fun because it means that you get to treat yourself! When you create your plan i.e. the pigeon steps you must take in order to get to your goal; create a reward system. At the end of each intermediate or major goal, treat yourself to an experience, food, or a time to relax so that you reconnect with life. My friend is very good at doing this. She would celebrate anything once she had achieved something, no matter how small. The great thing about it is that not only is she driven, I believe it has created a vibrancy and colourful animation in her life, and this is what it can do for you. Here's an example of what you might do "My goal is to feed 10 homeless people in central London right after work in one week. I'll reward myself to *Nando's* with my friends once complete." Very simple but effective if done properly. Please note, this requires discipline and does not require you to ignore the goal and go straight for *Nando's*, it requires you to make an attempt. If you have never ever achieved your goal before but you missed your target, the question is do you still treat yourself? That is dependent upon you, maybe you need to lower your target and re-evaluate, perhaps you don't want to treat yourself until you reach your goal. Whatever standards you create for your reward system, remember measure the deservedness of receiving your reward via your efforts and results. Effort is measured upon what you do to position yourself for success, and checking and looking at the habits you need in order to be successful. If your actions match 80% of those success habits, your efforts are very good, any less signifies the need for improvements. Regardless have fun creating your rewards system, and don't be too stingy on yourself!

A PERSONAL NOTE

I assume that by reading this book you are committed to achieving more in life. As you can see, the teachings in this book are not necessarily ground-breaking or revolutionary; rather they are things that work when the right set of attitudes have been employed in your mental framework. I truly believe that if you are determined enough to change your life positively and progressively towards your desired goals, then you will achieve heights that may even surpass your original vision. A result is a validation point for the brain, and emphasises and encourages the fact that more is possible; so aim to get them!

As constructive, positive and helpful ambassadors to each other, if you found the information within this book to be useful, I would very much be grateful if you post a short review on Amazon. Your message and support will really make a huge difference for helping others to decide to take action, in addition to, using constructive feedback to make this book even better for future readers.

If you'd like to leave a review, then all you need to do is go to Amazon and search for *Desire: The Cornerstone between nothing and Success* and leave a review under the **Customer reviews** section and click on the button **Write a customer review**.

Thanks again for your support!

ABOUT THE AUTHOR

MICHAEL TABIRADE is an enthusiastic and pragmatic Business & Life Strategist. He focuses on strategic positioning and behaviour change to adopt a positive impact. Based in London and growing up as a millennial, Michael has been able to learn and manifest these techniques into the NHS, having a proven track record for improving people, teams and services. Connect with Michael via the following social media platforms:

Fb – Michael Tabirade – Achieve More Success
Tw - @Mike_Tabirade
In - @Mike_Tabirade

Learn more about Michael and what he does at http://michaeltabirade.com

RESOURCES FROM MICHAEL

Book 1 -
Understand Reach Expand: 15 Super Effective ways to
Manage your Mind

5 Models for Success Mastery -
http://michaeltabirade.com/success-mastery-video-series/

100 ways to Be Positive -
http://michaeltabirade.com/100-ways-to-be-positive/

The 15 Cornerstones for Success

1. *Discover the Power of Passion*
2. *Follow the Patterns of Success*
3. *Unleash your Superpowers*
4. *Always go Above and Beyond*
5. *Turn your Wants into Needs*
6. *Cut out the crap and Focus*
7. *Master Concentration*
8. *Desire Drives Purpose*
9. *Acquire Strength*
10. *Develop a Winning Attitude*
11. *Run with your Dreams*
12. *Find Food and Eat!*
13. *Learn the Art of Endurance*
14. *Give your Life meaning*
15. *Satisfy your Expectations*

www.ingramcontent.com/pod-product-compliance
Lightning Source LLC
Chambersburg PA
CBHW050548280326
41933CB00011B/1766